Inside the Mind of Stephen Hawking

Quotes from a Scientific Genius

FRANK JOHNSON

CONTENTS

DISCLAIMER

All quotes within this book are in the words of Stephen Hawking. Although every effort has been taken to ensure the accuracy of all text, the author apologises in the event of any mistakes.

INTRODUCTION

It is rare that a scientist's reputation transcends the world of science so much as to become a household name. Stephen Hawking, however, is one such example.

Hawking's achievements are made all the more remarkable by the fact that he has been almost entirely paralysed for many years, having been diagnosed with motor neuron disease at the age of twenty-one. In spite of this debilitating condition, he has become a prolific author of books and scientific papers. He is celebrated for his ability to translate complicated scientific concepts into language that is accessible to the average person.

Widely regarded as one of the top physicists of modern times, Hawking has made revolutionary discoveries in the area of cosmology and specifically black holes.

Much of Hawking's appeal also comes from his keen sense of humour and his light-hearted outlook on life. He has made many TV appearances, including several documentaries, The Simpsons, and, recently on Monty Python Live (Mostly).

Although I have included a chapter on God and Religion, this is not intended to present Hawking in any way as a theist, or even a deist. Although he does not rule out the existence of a God, Hawking is certainly not religious; however his views on God are interesting and I have included the chapter for this reason alone.

This book contains some of Hawking's views on a variety of topics in order to give an insight into the mind of this scientific genius.

ABOUT HIMSELF

A Learn from mistakes

"I used to think information was destroyed in black hole. This was my biggest blunder, or at least my biggest blunder in science."

*

"I don't want to write an autobiography because I would become public property with no privacy left."

*

"In my school, the brightest boys did math and physics, the less bright did physics and chemistry, and the least bright did biology. I wanted to do math and physics, but my father made me do chemistry because he thought there would be no jobs for mathematicians."

*

"I hope I have helped to raise the profile of science and to show that physics is not a mystery but can be understood by ordinary people."

*

"My wife and I love each other very much."

*

"I am in touch with a company that hopes to replicate my voice. However, they are not replicating my original voice - if they did that, I would sound like a man in his 20s, which would be very strange! They are actually trying to replicate the synthesizer that sits on my wheelchair."

*

"I had a bet with Gordon Kane of Michigan University that the Higgs particle wouldn't be found."

*

"What I'd really like to control is not machines, but people."

*

"I have wondered about time all my life."

*

"Among physicists, I'm respected I hope."

*

"I first had the idea of writing a popular book about the universe in 1982. My intention was partly to earn money to pay my daughter's school fees."

*

"I was born on January 8, 1942, exactly three hundred years after the death of Galileo. I estimate, however, that about two hundred thousand other babies were also born that day. I don't know whether any of them was later interested in astronomy."

*

"As a child, I wanted to know how things worked and to control them. With a friend, I built a number of complicated models that I could control."

*

"Keeping an active mind has been vital to my survival, as has been maintaining a sense of humor."

*

"I have so much that I want to do. I hate wasting time."

*

"It is no good getting furious if you get stuck. What I do is keep thinking about the problem but work on something else. Sometimes it is years before I see the way forward. In the case of information loss and black holes, it was 29 years."

*

"My father was a research scientist in tropical medicine, so I always assumed I would be a scientist, too. I felt that medicine was too vague and inexact, so I chose physics."

*

"I had not expected 'A Brief History of Time' to be a best seller."

*

"I'm not afraid of death, but I'm in no hurry to die. I have so much I want to do first."

*

"I have visited Japan several times and have always been shown wonderful hospitality."

*

"I'm never any good in the morning. It is only after four in the afternoon that I get going."

*

"I was not a good student. I did not spend much time at college; I was too busy enjoying myself."

*

"It's a pity that nobody has found an exploding black hole. If they had, I would have won a Nobel prize."

*

"I am just a child who has never grown up. I still keep asking these 'how' and 'why' questions. Occasionally, I find an answer."

*

"If I had to choose a superhero to be, I would pick Superman. He's everything that I'm not."

*

"If I had a time machine, I'd visit Marilyn Monroe in her prime or drop in on Galileo as he turned his telescope to the heavens."

*

"I was never top of the class at school, but my classmates must have seen potential in me, because my nickname was 'Einstein.'"

*

"I grew up thinking that a research scientist was a natural thing to be."

*

"I entered the health care debate in response to a statement in the United States press in summer 2009 which claimed the National Health Service in Great Britain would have killed me off, were I a British citizen. I felt compelled to make a statement to explain the error."

*

"I have a full and satisfying life. My work and my family are very important to me."

*

"'The Simpsons' appearances were great fun. But I don't take them too seriously. I think 'The Simpsons' have treated my disability responsibly."

*

"I enjoy all forms of music - pop, classical and opera."

*

"Using e-mail, I can communicate with scientists all over the world."

*

"My goal is simple. It is a complete understanding of the universe, why it is as it is and why it exists at all."

*

"I want my books sold on airport bookstalls."

*

"I wouldn't be here today if it were not for the NHS. I have received a large amount of high-quality treatment without which I would not have survived."

*

"My first popular book, 'A Brief History of Time,' aroused a great deal of interest, but many found it difficult to understand."

*

"The voice I use is a very old hardware speech synthesizer made in 1986. I keep it because I have not heard a voice I like better and because I have identified with it."

*

"I have wanted to fly into space for many years, but never imagined it would really be feasible."

*

"It is extremely important to me to write for children."

*

"I don't care much for equations myself. This is partly because it is difficult for me to write them down, but mainly because I don't have an intuitive feeling for equations."

*

"I want to know why the universe exists, why there is something greater than nothing."

*

"Perhaps one day I will go into space."

.

ABOUT WOMEN

"In the past, there was active discrimination against women in science. That has now gone, and although there are residual effects, these are not enough to account for the small numbers of women, particularly in mathematics and physics."

*

"It is generally recognised that women are better than men at languages, personal relations and multi-tasking, but less good at map-reading and spatial awareness. It is therefore not unreasonable to suppose that women might be less good at mathematics and physics."

*

"Women. They are a complete mystery."

*

"While physics and mathematics may tell us how the universe began, they are not much use in predicting human behavior because there are far too many equations to solve. I'm no better than anyone else at understanding what makes people tick, particularly women."

SCIENCE & MATHS

"There could be shadow galaxies, shadow stars, and even shadow people."

*

"As Irving Good realised in 1965, machines with superhuman intelligence could repeatedly improve their design even further, triggering what Vernor Vinge called a 'singularity.'"

*

"I would like nuclear fusion to become a practical power source. It would provide an inexhaustible supply of energy, without pollution or global warming."

*

"Most sets of values would give rise to universes that, although they might be very beautiful, would contain no one able to wonder at that beauty."

*

"Time travel was once considered scientific heresy, and I used to avoid talking about it for fear of being labelled a 'crank.'"

*

"Even if it turns out that time travel is impossible, it is important that we understand why it is impossible."

*

"Earth might one day soon resemble the planet Venus."

*

"Because there is a law such as gravity, the universe can and will create itself from nothing."

*

"The universe is governed by science. But science tells us that we can't solve the equations, directly in the abstract."

*

"The usual approach of science of constructing a mathematical model cannot answer the questions of why there should be a universe for the model to describe. Why does the universe go to all the bother of existing?"

*

"The media need superheroes in science just as in every sphere of life, but there is really a continuous range of abilities with no clear dividing line."

*

"Time can behave like another direction in space under extreme conditions."

*

"It was Einstein's dream to discover the grand design of the universe, a single theory that explains everything. However, physicists in Einstein's day hadn't made enough progress in understanding the forces of nature for that to be a realistic goal."

*

"The radiation left over from the Big Bang is the same as that in your microwave oven but very much less powerful. It would heat your pizza only to minus 271.3*C - not much good for defrosting the pizza, let alone cooking it."

*

"Scientists have become the bearers of the torch of discovery in our quest for knowledge."

*

"Science is beautiful when it makes simple explanations of phenomena or connections between different observations. Examples include the double helix in biology and the fundamental equations of physics."

*

"A zero-gravity flight is a first step toward space travel."

*

"No one undertakes research in physics with the intention of winning a prize. It is the joy of discovering something no one knew before."

*

"With genetic engineering, we will be able to increase the complexity of our DNA, and improve the human race. But it will be a slow process, because one will have to wait about 18 years to see the effect of changes to the genetic code."

*

"If we do discover a complete theory, it should be in time understandable in broad principle by everyone. Then we shall all, philosophers, scientists, and just ordinary people be able to take part in the discussion of why we and the universe exist."

*

"There is a real danger that computers will develop intelligence and take over. We urgently need to develop direct connections to the brain so that computers can add to human intelligence rather than be in opposition."

*

"Our minds work in real time, which begins at the Big Bang and will end, if there is a Big Crunch - which seems unlikely, now, from the latest data showing accelerating expansion. Consciousness would come to an end at a singularity."

*

"I think the discovery of supersymmetric partners for the known particles would revolutionize our understanding of the universe."

*

"The fastest manned vehicle in history was Apollo 10. It reached 25,000 mph."

*

"Science is not only a disciple of reason but, also, one of romance and passion."

*

"If you believe in science, like I do, you believe that there are certain laws that are always obeyed."

*

"One cannot really argue with a mathematical theorem."

*

"Throughout history, people have studied pure science from a desire to understand the universe rather than practical applications for commercial gain. But their discoveries later turned out to have great practical benefits."

*

"The Planck satellite may detect the imprint of the gravitational waves predicted by inflation. This would be quantum gravity written across the sky."

*

"Evolution has ensured that our brains just aren't equipped to visualise 11 dimensions directly. However, from a purely mathematical point of view it's just as easy to think in 11 dimensions, as it is to think in three or four."

*

"As scientists, we step on the shoulders of science, building on the work that has come before us - aiming to inspire a new generation of young scientists to continue once we are gone."

*

"There are plenty of dead scientists I admire, but I can't think of any living ones. This is probably because it is only in retrospect that one can see who made the important contributions."

*

"When we understand string theory, we will know how the universe began. It won't have much effect on how we live, but it is important to understand where we come from and what we can expect to find as we explore."

*

"Up until the 1920s, everyone thought the universe was essentially static and unchanging in time."

*

"Before 1915, space and time were thought of as a fixed arena in which events took place, but which was not affected by what happened in it. Space and time are now dynamic quantities... space and time not only affect but are also affected by everything that happens in the universe."

*

"Only black holes of very low mass would emit a significant amount of radiation."

*

"Some people would claim that things like love, joy and beauty belong to a different category from science and can't be described in scientific terms, but I think they can now be explained by the theory of evolution."

*

"Time travel used to be thought of as just science fiction, but Einstein's general theory of relativity allows for the possibility that we could warp space-time so much that you could go off in a rocket and return before you set out."

*

"Observations indicate that the universe is expanding at an ever increasing rate. It will expand forever, getting emptier and darker."

*

"There is nothing bigger or older than the universe."

*

"Imaginary time is a new dimension, at right angles to ordinary, real time."

*

"The cyclic universe theory predicts no gravitational waves from the early universe."

*

"To my mathematical brain, the numbers alone make thinking about aliens perfectly rational. The real challenge is to work out what aliens might actually be like."

*

"Science predicts that many different kinds of universe will be spontaneously created out of nothing. It is a matter of chance which we are in."

*

"For years, my early work with Roger Penrose seemed to be a disaster for science. It showed that the universe must have begun with a singularity, if Einstein's general theory of relativity is correct. That appeared to indicate that science could not predict how the universe would begin."

*

 "According to 'M' theory, ours is not the only universe. Instead, 'M' theory predicts that a great many universes were created out of nothing."

*

"It now appears that the way the universe began can indeed be determined, using imaginary time."

*

"Some scientists think it may be possible to capture a wormhole and enlarge it many trillions of times to make it big enough for a human or even a spaceship to enter."

*

"If we want to travel into the future, we just need to go fast. Really fast. And I think the only way we're ever likely to do that is by going into space."

*

 "Science can lift people out of poverty and cure disease. That, in turn, will reduce civil unrest."

*

"My discovery that black holes emit radiation raised serious problems of consistency with the rest of physics. I have now resolved these problems, but the answer turned out to be not what I expected."

*

"Most people don't have time to master the very mathematical details of theoretical physics."

*

"The missing link in cosmology is the nature of dark matter and dark energy."

*

"There is no physical law precluding particles from being organised in ways that perform even more advanced computations than the arrangements of particles in human brains."

*

"M-theory is the unified theory Einstein was hoping to find."

*

"I believe there are no questions that science can't answer about a physical universe."

*

"Although almost every theoretical physicist agrees with my prediction that a black hole should glow like a hot body, it would be very difficult to verify experimentally because the temperature of a macroscopic black hole is so low."

*

"If the rate of expansion one second after the Big Bang had been smaller by even one part in a hundred thousand million million, it would have recollapsed before it reached its present size. On the other hand, if it had been greater by a part in a million, the universe would have expanded too rapidly for stars and planets to form."

*

"We think that life develops spontaneously on Earth, so it must be possible for life to develop on suitable planets elsewhere in the universe. But we don't know the probability that a planet develops life."

*

"Cosmology is a rapidly advancing field."

DISABILITY

"Maybe I don't have the most common kind of motor neuron disease, which usually kills in two or three years."

*

"Some forms of motor neuron disease are genetically linked, but I have no indication that my kind is. No other member of my family has had it. But I would be in favour of abortion if there was a high risk."

*

"Sometimes I wonder if I'm as famous for my wheelchair and disabilities as I am for my discoveries."

*

"I don't have much positive to say about motor neuron disease, but it taught me not to pity myself because others were worse off, and to get on with what I still could do. I'm happier now than before I developed the condition."

*

"Stem cell research is the key to developing cures for degenerative conditions like Parkinson's and motor neuron disease from which I and many others suffer. The fact that the cells may come from embryos is not an objection, because the embryos are going to die anyway."

*

"The doctor who diagnosed me with ALS, or motor neuron disease, told me that it would kill me in two or three years."

*

"I can't say that my disability has helped my work, but it has allowed me to concentrate on research without having to lecture or sit on boring committees."

*

"Theoretical physics is one of the few fields in which being disabled is no handicap - it is all in the mind."

*

"My advice to other disabled people would be, concentrate on things your disability doesn't prevent you doing well, and don't regret the things it interferes with. Don't be disabled in spirit as well as physically."

*

"Obviously, because of my disability, I need assistance. But I have always tried to overcome the limitations of my condition and lead as full a life as possible. I have traveled the world, from the Antarctic to zero gravity."

*

"The Paralympic Games is about transforming our perception of the world."

*

"I think those who have a terminal illness and are in great pain should have the right to choose to end their own life, and those that help them should be free from prosecution."

GENERAL THOUGHTS & OPINIONS

"There are grounds for cautious optimism that we may now be near the end of the search for the ultimate laws of nature."

*

"People won't have time for you if you are always angry or complaining."

*

"There are too many accidents that can befall life on a single planet."

*

"Wagner manages to convey emotion with music
better than anyone, before or since."

*

"We live in a bewildering world."

*

"I think the brain is essentially a computer and
consciousness is like a computer program. It will
cease to run when the computer is turned off.
Theoretically, it could be re-created on a neural
network, but that would be very difficult, as it
would require all one's memories."

*

"The past, like the future, is indefinite and exists
only as a spectrum of possibilities."

*

"I believe things cannot make themselves impossible."

*

"I have found far greater enthusiasm for science in America than here in Britain. There is more enthusiasm for everything in America."

*

"Many badly needed goals, like fusion and cancer cure, would be achieved much sooner if we invested more."

*

"Cambridge is one of the best universities in the world, especially in my field."

*

"If aliens visit us, the outcome would be much as

when Columbus landed in America, which didn't turn out well for the Native Americans."

*

"Exploration by real people inspires us."

*

"I believe in universal health care. And I am not afraid to say so."

*

"Life on Earth is at the ever-increasing risk of being wiped out by a disaster, such as sudden global nuclear war, a genetically engineered virus or other dangers we have not yet thought of."

*

"I think it quite likely that we are the only civilization within several hundred light years; otherwise we would have heard radio waves."

*

"If you understand the universe, you control it, in a way."

*

"Many people find the universe confusing - it's not."

*

"You can't regulate every lab in the world."

*

"I believe everyone should have a broad picture of how the universe operates and our place in it. It is a basic human desire. And it also puts our worries in perspective."

*

"In Britain, like most of the developed world, stem-cell research is regarded as a great opportunity. America will be left behind if it doesn't change policy."

*

"Success in creating AI would be the biggest event in human history. Unfortunately, it might also be the last, unless we learn how to avoid the risks."

*

"Although September 11 was horrible, it didn't threaten the survival of the human race, like nuclear weapons do."

*

"It is not clear that intelligence has any long-term survival value."

GOD & RELIGION

"So long as the universe had a beginning, we could suppose it had a creator. But if the universe is really completely self-contained, having no boundary or edge, it would have neither beginning nor end: it would simply be. What place, then, for a creator?"

*

"Not only does God play dice, but... he sometimes throws them where they cannot be seen."

*

"The whole history of science has been the gradual

realization that events do not happen in an arbitrary manner, but that they reflect a certain underlying order, which may or may not be divinely inspired."

*

 "There is no heaven or afterlife for broken-down computers; that is a fairy story for people afraid of the dark."

*

"I believe the universe is governed by the laws of science. The laws may have been decreed by God, but God does not intervene to break the laws."

*

"God is the name people give to the reason we are here. But I think that reason is the laws of physics rather than someone with whom one can have a personal relationship. An impersonal God."

*

"What was God doing before the divine creation?"

*

 "Theology is unnecessary."

*

"Science is increasingly answering questions that used to be the province of religion."

HUMOROUS

"I can't disguise myself with a wig and dark glasses
- the wheelchair gives me away."

*

"No one can resist the idea of a crippled genius."

*

"Someone told me that each equation I included in
the book would halve the sales."

*

"We think we have solved the mystery of creation.
Maybe we should patent the universe and charge
everyone royalties for their existence."

*

"I believe alien life is quite common in the universe,
although intelligent life is less so. Some say it has
yet to appear on planet Earth."

MANKIND

"I have noticed even people who claim everything is predestined, and that we can do nothing to change it, look before they cross the road."

*

"People who boast about their I.Q. are losers."

*

"In less than a hundred years, we have found a new way to think of ourselves. From sitting at the center of the universe, we now find ourselves orbiting an average-sized sun, which is just one of millions of stars in our own Milky Way galaxy."

*

"I don't think the human race will survive the next thousand years, unless we spread into space."

*

"We are in danger of destroying ourselves by our greed and stupidity. We cannot remain looking inwards at ourselves on a small and increasingly polluted and overcrowded planet."

*

"I think the human race doesn't have a future if it doesn't go into space."

*

"We are just an advanced breed of monkeys on a minor planet of a very average star. But we can understand the Universe. That makes us something very special."

*

"We are all different. There is no such thing as a standard or run-of-the-mill human being, but we share the same human spirit."

*

"The human race may be the only intelligent beings in the galaxy."

*

"We only have to look at ourselves to see how intelligent life might develop into something we wouldn't want to meet."

*

"We are the product of quantum fluctuations in the very early universe."

*

"I think computer viruses should count as life. I think it says something about human nature that the only form of life we have created so far is purely destructive. We've created life in our own image."

*

"Our population and our use of the finite resources of planet Earth are growing exponentially, along with our technical ability to change the environment for good or ill."

*

"I think we have a good chance of surviving long enough to colonize the solar system."

PHILOSOPHY

"To confine our attention to terrestrial matters
would be to limit the human spirit."

*

"Life would be tragic if it weren't funny."

*

"When one's expectations are reduced to zero, one
really appreciates everything one does have."

*

"A few years ago, the city council of Monza, Italy, barred pet owners from keeping goldfish in curved bowls... saying that it is cruel to keep a fish in a bowl with curved sides because, gazing out, the fish would have a distorted view of reality. But how do we know we have the true, undistorted picture of reality?"

*

 "Nothing cannot exist forever."

*

"Why are we here? Where do we come from? Traditionally, these are questions for philosophy, but philosophy is dead."

*

"Work gives you meaning and purpose and life is empty without it."

*

"There is no unique picture of reality."

*

"We should seek the greatest value of our action."

*

"Look up at the stars and not down at your feet. Try to make sense of what you see, and wonder about what makes the universe exist. Be curious."

*

"Even if there is only one possible unified theory, it is just a set of rules and equations. What is it that breathes fire into the equations and makes a universe for them to describe?"

*

"There's no way to remove the observer - us - from our perceptions of the world."

*

"Philosophers have not kept up with modern developments in science. Particularly physics."

*

"Intelligence is the ability to adapt to change."

*

"The universe is not indifferent to our existence - it depends on it."

*

"One can't predict the weather more than a few days in advance."

*

"However difficult life may seem, there is always something you can do and succeed at."

ALSO BY FRANK JOHNSON

INSIDE THE MIND OF CHUCK PALAHNIUK

THE WIT AND WISDOM OF JOSS WHEDON

INSIDE THE MIND OF EMMA WATSON

THE VERY BEST OF MICHAEL MOORE

THE PHILOSOPHY OF PAUL WATSON

Printed in Great Britain
by Amazon.co.uk, Ltd.,
Marston Gate.